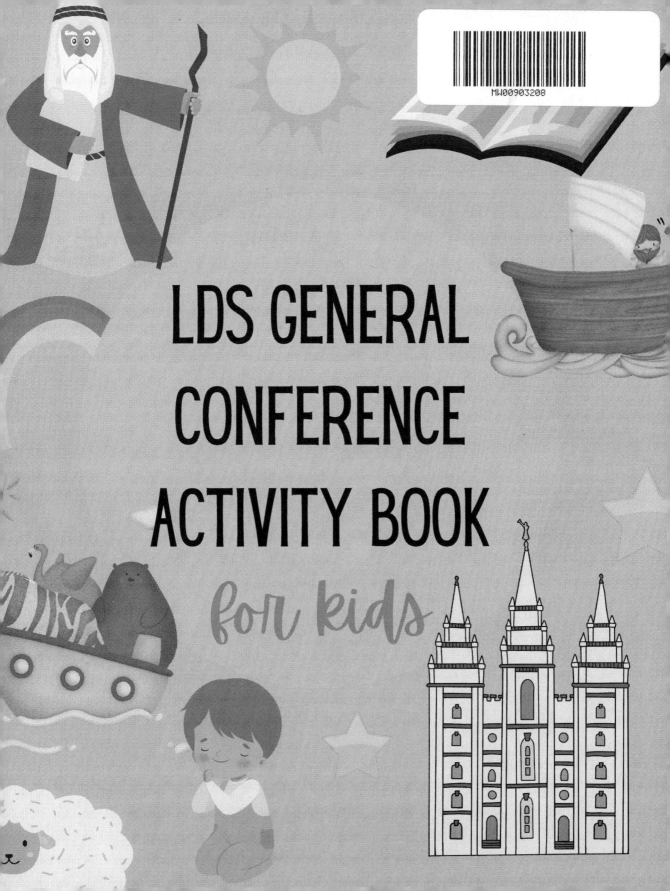

LDS GENERAL CONFERENCE ACTIVITY BOOK

for kids

THIS BOOK BELONGS TO

_____

GENERAL CONFERENCE ACTIVITY BOOK FOR KIDS

This book will help kids stay engaged while listening to The Church of Jesus Christ of Latter-day Saints Semi-Annual General Conferences. The pages can be completed in order or they can be done out of order.

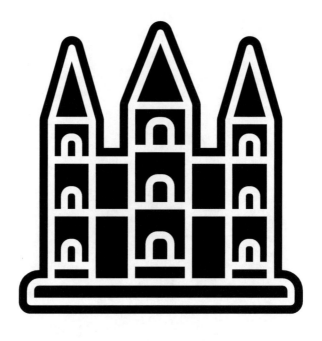

Color the speaker's tie.

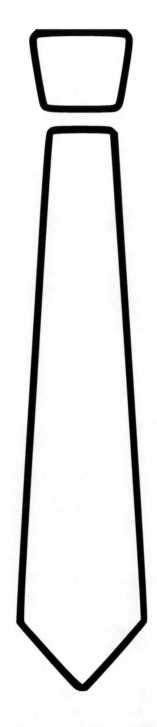

Color the hearts or write words from this talk that stand out to you inside the hearts.

SPEAKER NAME _____

Write or draw what the speaker is talking about.

SPEAKER NAME _____

Color each petal once you hear the word on it.

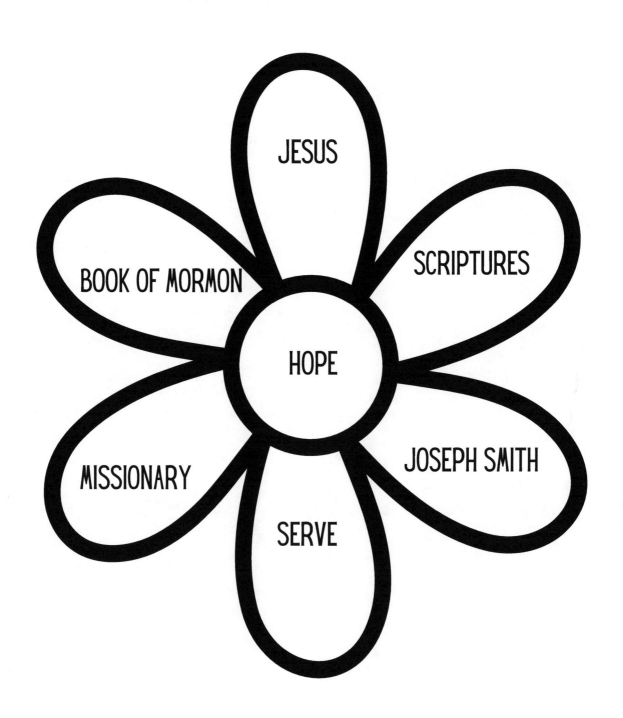

Find your way through the maze!

SPEAKER NAME _____

How can you apply what speaker is talking about to your life?

Color the picture below while listening to the speaker.

I'm so glad I live in this beautiful world.

Color the picture below.

Color the
picture when
you hear the
word inside it.

SPEAKER NAME _____

Find the hidden words. Words are hidden up, down, & diagonal.

```
Q  S  I  W  G  G  F  X  F  D
U  C  M  S  Z  W  F  K  A  W
T  R  T  E  T  W  C  V  I  K
L  I  J  R  K  D  V  V  T  R
O  P  I  V  N  W  X  S  H  B
V  T  X  E  C  H  U  R  C  H
E  U  I  M  N  S  Y  F  S  Y
P  R  A  Y  E  O  N  U  M  R
F  E  U  J  G  K  I  N  D  C
V  S  Z  B  H  Y  M  N  S  E
```

JESUS	KIND	SERVE
LOVE	FAITH	FRIEND
SCRIPTURES	HYMNS	PRAY
CHURCH		

If you earn 10 dollars, how much tithing should you pay?
Color tithing yellow and other dollars green.

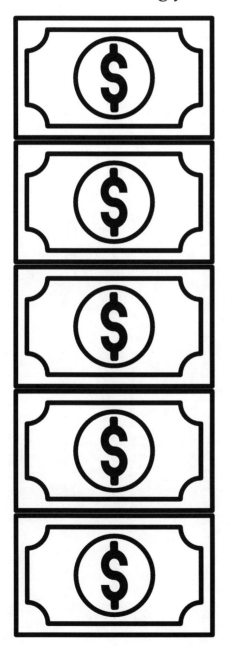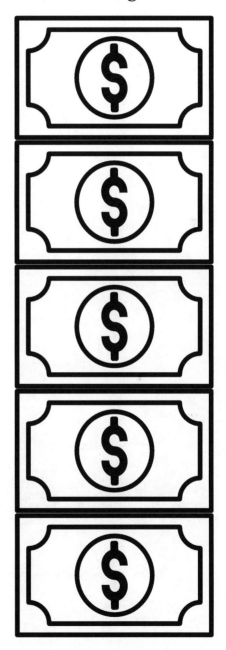

Find your way through the maze!

As for me and my house, we will serve the Lord.
-Joshua 24:15

Color the speaker's top.

Find your way through the maze!

When you need help in your life – pray!

Color the fish
when you hear
the word inside it
spoken.

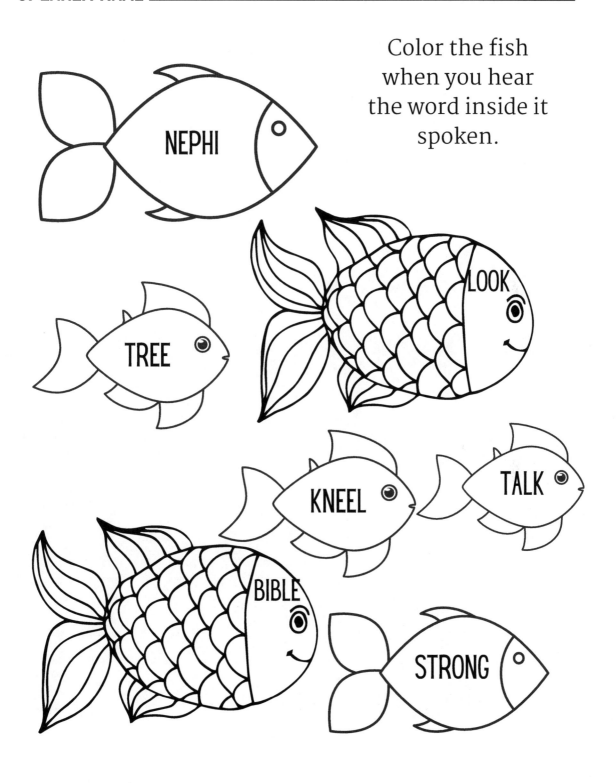

SPEAKER NAME _____

Write or draw what the speaker is talking about.

Write or draw kind things you can do for others on the hearts below.

I am kind.

Color the speaker's tie.

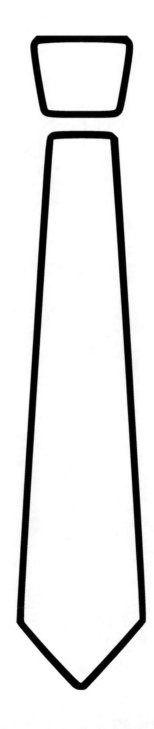

Find your way through the maze!

A new commandment I give unto you, that ye love one another
-John 13:34

Find the hidden words. Words are hidden up, down, & diagonal.

```
L  I  S  T  E  N  M  A  F  M
Z  T  E  M  P  L  E  P  Q  I
P  R  O  P  H  E  T  O  Q  S
H  P  I  Q  P  H  A  S  Y  S
W  H  C  Q  M  S  D  T  V  I
I  I  N  V  I  T  E  L  Y  O
P  R  I  M  A  R  Y  E  H  N
I  S  I  N  G  Q  X  S  P  U
Z  V  N  D  S  P  I  R  I  T
Z  B  A  P  T  I  S  M  F  P
```

PROPHET	APOSTLES	LISTEN
TEMPLE	BAPTISM	SPIRIT
MISSION	SING	PRIMARY
INVITE		

SPEAKER NAME _____

Color each puzzle piece as you hear the word inside it.

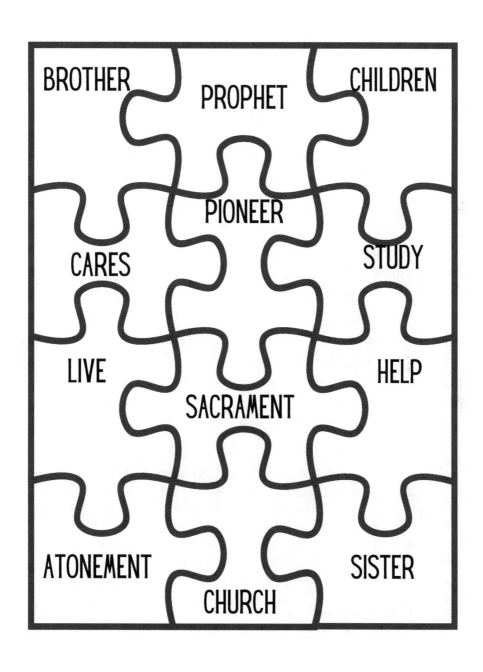

SPEAKER NAME _____

How can you apply what speaker is talking about to your life?

Color this scripture from 1 Nephi 3:7.

I will go and do the things which the Lord hath commanded.

Color this picture while you listen to the speaker.

Write your favorite primary songs or hymns on the notes
below or color the notes.

SPEAKER NAME _____

Write or draw what the speaker is talking about.

SPEAKER NAME _____

Color each animal as you hear the word inside it.

LEADER

NEW
TESTAMENT

PARENTS

LOVE

Color the speaker's top.

Color the picture of the empty tomb below.

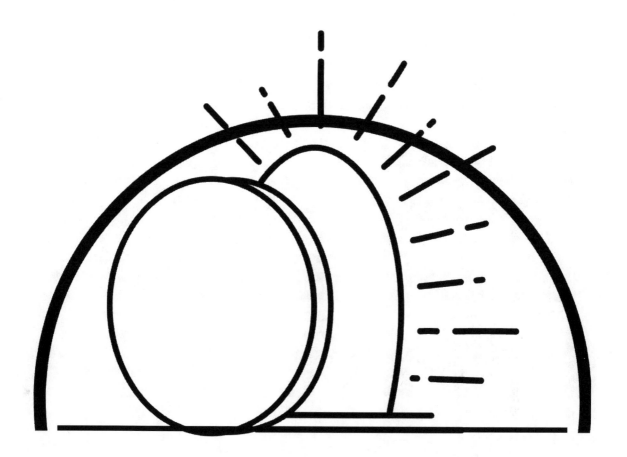

Tomb

Complete the maze below.

Color the rainbow.

I like to look for rainbows.

Complete the maze below.

Match the prophet with the corresponding picture.

Noah

Nephi

Moses

Jonah

David

How can you apply what speaker is talking about to your life?

Color this scripture from Proverbs 3:5-6.

TRUST IN THE LORD WITH ALL YOUR HEART AND LEAN NOT UNTO THINE OWN UNDERSTANDING

SPEAKER NAME _____

Do you know anyone who has served a mission? Write their name on the globe below where they served. Write your name where you would choose to go on a mission. Color the picture.

I CAN BE A MISSIONARY NOW

SPEAKER NAME _____

Draw a picture or write things you are grateful for.

Color Noah's Ark while listening to the speaker.

Color the speaker's tie.

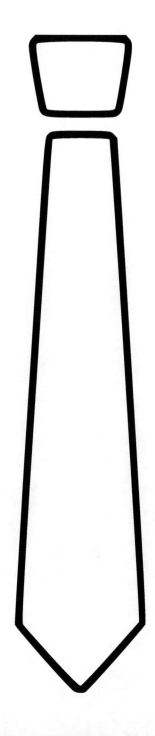

SPEAKER NAME _____

Write or draw what the speaker is talking about.

Color the picture & write how you know Jesus loves you.

I know Jesus loves me because...

SPEAKER NAME _____

Find the hidden words. Words are hidden up, down, & diagonal.

```
Q V R B Z S J S X S Y Q M B X
C K Z Z W J O A S A L M A P K
J N E P H I O B O C N P U B X
A B D T Q N L S X K V Z Z O Q
J C U Y L G E A E C X W O O E
V R N E T S G W F P C V A K A
I A I U O X L S S J H M R F S
K P W M P K Z C N Q E U S V H
E D J T Y P E T E R D K I U W
N O H F K Z V V S A U X A B M
L E G I G V E I T D O U J Y C
V G Z S K I W V H A M Z A J I
S N Q M F C P P E M O R O N I
Z D V R V Y W B R J B S E Y E
X I Q S X Z G A C R Y Q X B U
```

NEPHI	ALMA	MORONI
ADAM	EVE	ESTHER
MOSES	JOSEPH	RUTH
PETER		

Color the speaker's top.

Complete the maze below.

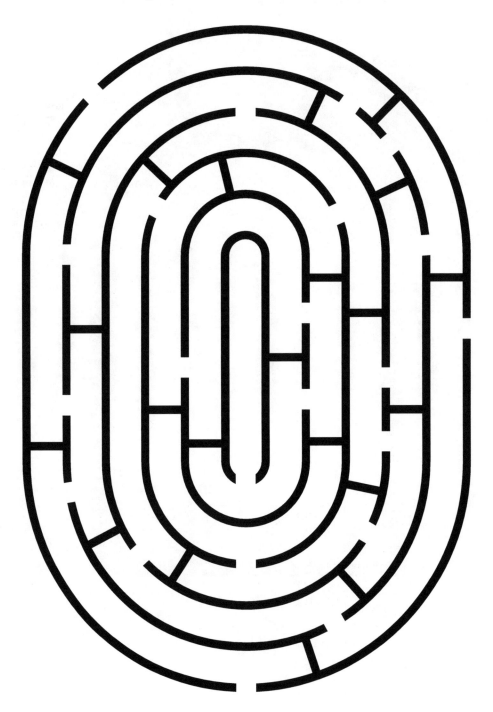

Color the sheep as you hear each word spoken inside of them.

Color a picture of yourself below & write your name on the blank line below. Write or draw your gifts or talents on the hearts.

Jesus love me,

☐☐☐☐☐☐☐☐☐☐

SPEAKER NAME _____

Write or color you favorite scripture story in the book below.

I love to read the
scriptures!

SPEAKER NAME _____

Draw a picture of your family.

Families can be together forever.

Color the children praying below while you listen to the speaker.

I kneel to pray every day.

Color each of the Easter eggs as you hear the word spoken inside it.

HEAVEN

GARDEN

APOSTLE

COVENANT

BAPTIZED

HOLY GHOST

Color the speaker's tie.

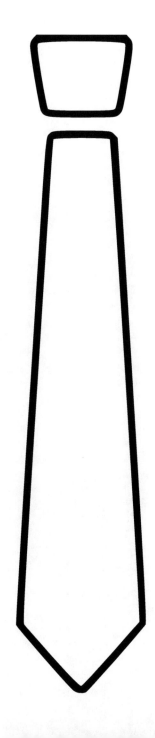

SPEAKER NAME _____

Write or draw what the speaker is talking about.

Color in these words as you listen to the prophet speak.

CONFERENCE FOLLOW-UP

What did you learn from conference? What was your
favorite talk? What is one thing you are going to apply?
Write or draw inside the hearts below.

IF YOU ENJOYED THIS BOOK, MAKE SURE TO LEAVE A REVIEW.

CHECK OUT OUR OTHER ACTIVITY BOOKS, JOURNALS, & STUDY GUIDES.

FOLLOW US ONLINE!

@LATTER.DAY.DESIGNS

LATTER-DAY DESIGNS

Made in United States
Troutdale, OR
04/04/2024